12-1-18
$27.04

D0855722

by Jim Gigliotti

Consultant: Craig Ellenport
Former Senior Editor
NFL.com

New York, New York

Credits

Cover, © Cal Sport Media/Alamy Stock Photo; 4, © Leslie Plaza Johnson/Icon Sportswire/Newscom; 4–5, © AP Photo/Pheban Ebenhack; 6, © Mark Alberti/Icon Sportswire/Newscom; 7, © Dwane Lindsey; 8, © NOW Publications; 9, © NOW Publications; 10, © Ken Wolter/Shutterstock; 11, © Rick Wood/MCT/Newscom; 12, © ZUMA Press Inc./Alamy Stock Photo; 12–13, © AP Photo/Aaron M. Sprecher; 14, © AP Photo/Rick Osentoski; 14–15, © AP Photo/Aaron M. Sprecher; 16, © Jeff Haynes/Reuters/Newscom; 16–17, © AP Photo/Matt Patterson; 18, © Sporting News/Newscom; 19, © AP Photo/Matt Patterson; 20, © Brett Coomer/Houston Chronicle via AP Photo; 21, © AP Photo/Aaron M. Sprecher; 22, © Leslie Plaza Johnson/Icon Sportswire/Newscom; 23T, © Daniel Thornberg/Dreamstime.com; 23B, © AP Photo/Rick Osentoski.

Publisher: Kenn Goin
Senior Editor: Joyce Tavolacci
Creative Director: Spencer Brinker
Production and Photo Research: Shoreline Publishing Group LLC

Library of Congress Cataloging-in-Publication Data

Names: Gigliotti, Jim, author.
Title: J.J. Watt / by Jim Gigliotti.
Description: New York, New York : Bearport Publishing, [2018] | Series: Amazing Americans: football stars | Includes bibliographical references and index.
Identifiers: LCCN 2017041479 (print) | LCCN 2017046767 (ebook) | ISBN 9781684025114 (ebook) | ISBN 9781684024537 (library)
Subjects: LCSH: Watt, J. J., 1989-–Juvenile literature. | Football players—United States—Biography—Juvenile literature.
Classification: LCC GV939.W362 (ebook) | LCC GV939.W362 G54 2018 (print) | DDC 796.332092 [B] —dc23
LC record available at https://lccn.loc.gov/2017041479

For more information, write to Bearport Publishing Company, Inc., 45 West 21st Street, Suite 3B, New York, New York 10010. Printed in the United States of America.

10 9 8 7 6 5 4 3 2 1

CONTENTS

Sack Time!

J.J. Watt raced down the field. Before any player could block him, he rushed toward the **quarterback**. *Slam!* J.J. knocked him over. That's just another **sack** for one of football's best **defensive** players!

J.J. Watt plays for the Houston Texans. His position is called defensive end.

J.J. tackles another player.

Young J.J.

Justin James "J.J." Watt was born on March 22, 1989, in Wisconsin. He grew up with two younger brothers. From an early age, J.J. and his brothers loved sports. J.J. dreamed of becoming a football player in the NFL.

J.J. and his brothers made a football field in their backyard.

T.J. Watt, J.J.'s brother, joined the Pittsburgh Steelers in 2017.

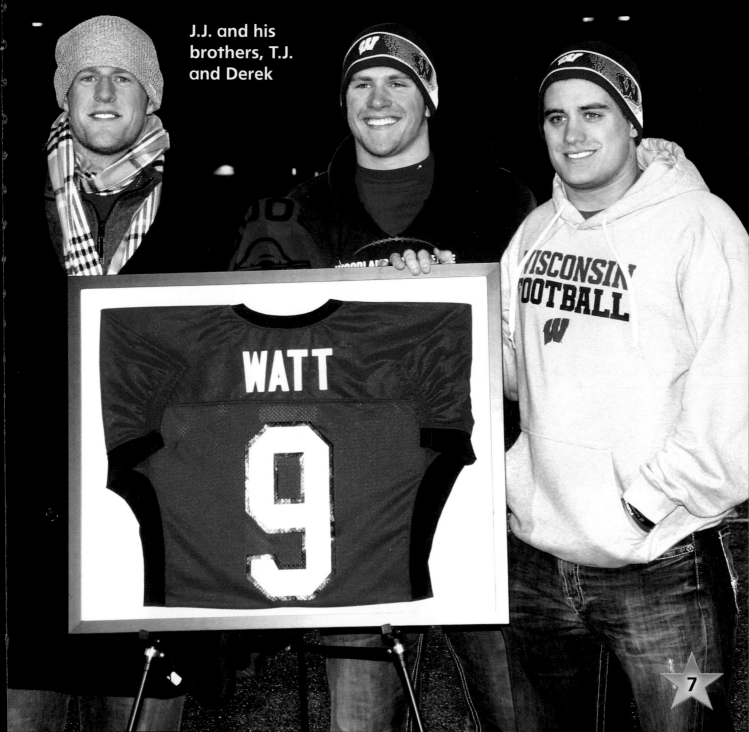

J.J. and his brothers, T.J. and Derek

WATT
9

Sports Star

In high school, J.J. joined the football team. He was strong and fast. This helped him play different positions, including **tight end** and defensive end. Soon, everyone began to notice his huge talent.

J.J. (#9) playing defensive end in high school

J.J. gets ready to dunk the ball.

J.J. was great at other sports, too. He was a basketball, baseball, and track-and-field star.

College Days

After high school, J.J. went to the University of Wisconsin. J.J. joined their football team and played his hardest. By 2010, he was Wisconsin's most valuable player (MVP)!

Bascom Hall at the University of Wisconsin

To help pay for college, J.J. got a job delivering pizzas.

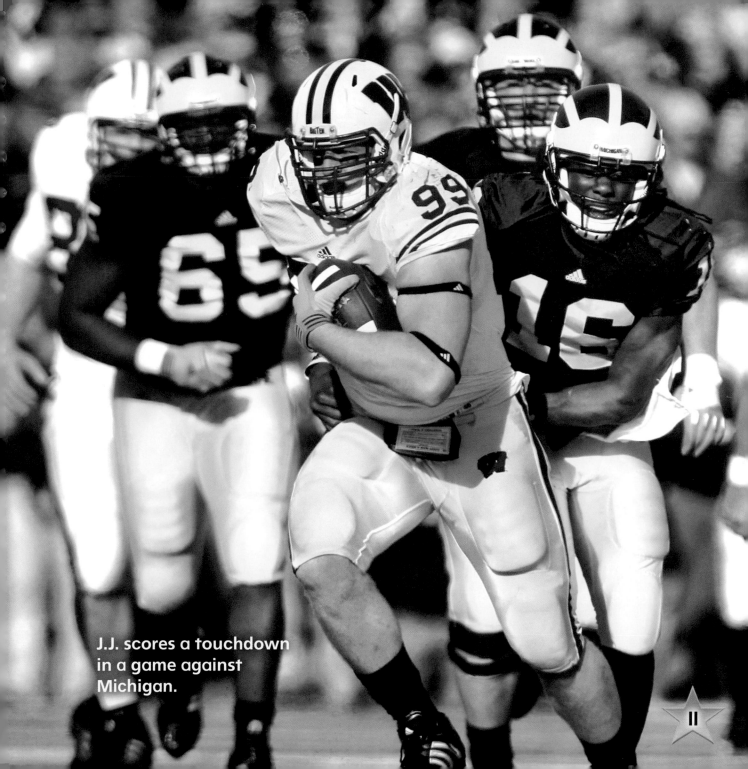

J.J. scores a touchdown in a game against Michigan.

Pro Player!

J.J. set his sights on the NFL. In 2011, the Houston Texans **drafted** him. On the field, J.J. didn't disappoint. He helped the Texans make the playoffs for the first time ever! "I had a dream and made it a goal," said J.J.

J.J.'s first sack was against New Orleans quarterback Drew Brees.

J.J. holds up his Texans jersey on draft day.

J.J. recovers a
fumble against the
Indianapolis Colts.

13

Second-Year Star

By 2012, J.J. had become one of the best players in the NFL. He led the league with 20.5 sacks! He also made the Pro Bowl—the NFL's all-star game. On top of that, J.J. was named the league's Defensive Player of the Year!

J.J.'s strength helps him make sack after sack.

With his arms up, J.J. gets ready to knock down a pass.

J.J. knocked down so many passes that fans began calling him "J.J. Swatt."

Unstoppable

In J.J.'s next three seasons, he had a total of 48.5 sacks! He was so strong that it took two or three players to block him. J.J. was named the NFL's Defensive Player of the Year two more times.

J.J. receiving his 2012 NFL Defensive Player of the Year Award

In 2014,
J.J. caught three
touchdown passes!

Fan Favorite

J.J. is known for more than his amazing football skills. Off the field, he enjoys working with kids. In 2011, he started the Justin J. Watt Foundation. The group provides sports programs for children.

At a Halloween party at a children's hospital, J.J. dressed up as Batman. He loves making kids smile!

J.J. greets fans during a softball game. The game raised money for his foundation.

"Dream Big!"

J.J. missed most of the 2016 season after hurting his back. Still, he remains one of America's favorite football stars. J.J. came back in 2017 to help his team play their best. As J.J. says, "Dream big, work hard!"

Hurricane Harvey hit Houston in 2017. J.J. helped raise $30 million for hurricane victims.

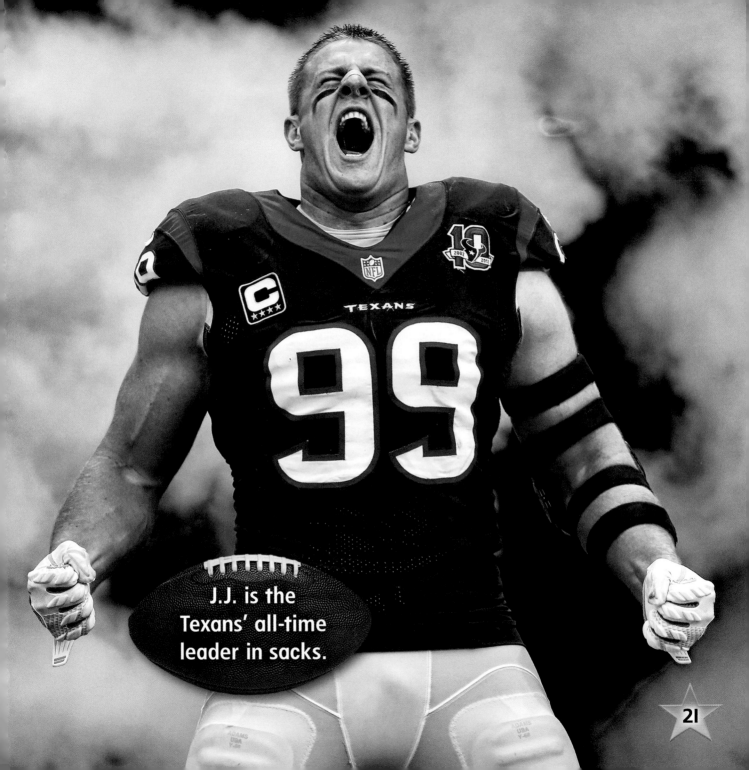

J.J. is the Texans' all-time leader in sacks.

Timeline

Here are some key dates in J.J. Watt's life.

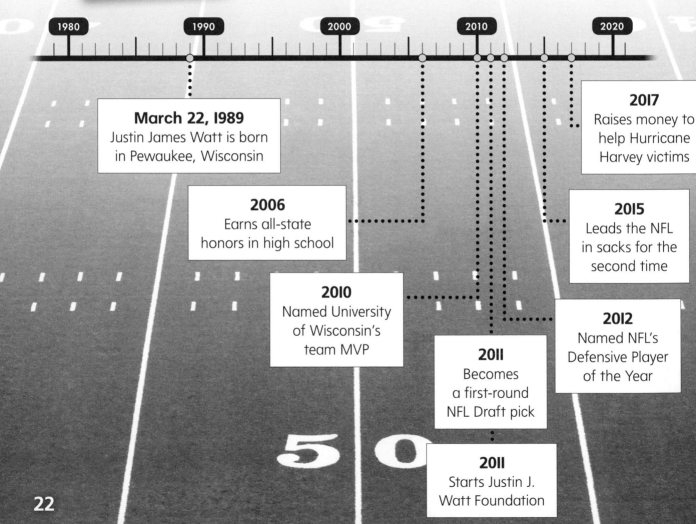

1980   1990   2000   2010   2020

March 22, 1989
Justin James Watt is born in Pewaukee, Wisconsin

2006
Earns all-state honors in high school

2010
Named University of Wisconsin's team MVP

2011
Becomes a first-round NFL Draft pick

2011
Starts Justin J. Watt Foundation

2017
Raises money to help Hurricane Harvey victims

2015
Leads the NFL in sacks for the second time

2012
Named NFL's Defensive Player of the Year

Glossary

defensive (dee-FEN-siv) acting to keep the team with the ball from scoring

drafted (DRAFT-id) chosen by an NFL team

quarterback (KWOR-tur-bak) a football player who leads the offense, the part of a team that moves the ball forward

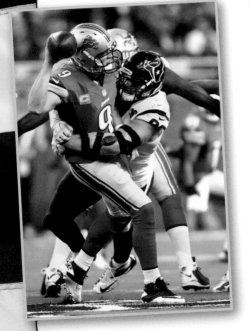

sack (SAK) a football play in which a player tackles the quarterback while he's trying to pass the ball

tight end (TITE END) an offensive player whose job is to both block and catch passes

Index

Read More

Kelley, K.C. *J.J. Watt (Football Stars Up Close).* New York: Bearport (2016).

Raum, Elizabeth. *J.J. Watt (Pro Sports Biographies).* Mankato, MN: Amicus Ink (2017).

Learn More Online

To learn more about J.J. Watt, visit
www.bearportpublishing.com/AmazingAmericans

About the Author

Jim Gigliotti is a former editor at the National Football League. He now writes books on a variety of topics for young readers.